GET UNSTUCK™

A Guide for Those Over 50

GET UNSTUCK™

A Guide for Those Over 50

by Andrew Pais,
MCHt, MNLP, MTT, MSC

Published by
RockStar Publishing House
28039 Smyth Drive
Suite 102
Valencia, CA 91355
www.rockstarpublishinghouse.com

Copyright © 2013 by Andrew Pais

All rights reserved. No part of this book may be reproduced or transmitted in any form or by in any means, electronic or mechanical, including photocopying, recording, or by any information storage and retrieval system, without the written permission of the Publisher, except where permitted by law.

Manufactured in the United States of America, or in the United Kingdom when distributed elsewhere.

Author Pais, Andrew
Get UnStuck
        Worthy Shorts ID: RSP201

ISBN:
Paperback: 978-1-937506-28-5
ePub: 978-1-937506-29-2
PDF: 978-1-937506-30-8

Excerpt from Healing the Mind and Body, by Paul D. Corona, M.D. © 2007. Reprinted by permission of the publisher, The Corona Mind-Body Institute.

Cover design by: Teagarden Designs
Interior design: Darlene Swanson

This book is based upon my journey and the outcomes are solely up to each individual to achieve.

www.americasunstuckcoach.com

Dedicated To:

Mr. Thomas Dixon Lovely, who started me on this journey back in Long Beach Junior High School more than 45 years ago.

The late Hank Giordano, my mentor, coach and best friend, who taught and showed by example how to really live life.

And especially Margie Carpenter, my friend and muse. Without her support and her constantly telling me "You can do it," this book wouldn't have happened.

Acknowledgements

To the people who inspired me, coached me, and got me unstuck:

Maurice DiMino

Michael Stevenson

Craig Duswalt

Ruben Mata

Kimberly Rinaldi

Michelle Gutman

Judy Brizendine

Debby Johnson

Kelly Chaplin

Eiji Morishita

Glenn Morshower

Sandra Dee Robinson

TABLE OF CONTENTS

	Introduction xiii
Part I:	My Path from Being Stuck to Getting Unstuck. 1
Part II:	How You Get Stuck 11
Part III:	How Does the Mind-Body Connection Really Work? . . . 27
Part IV:	Getting Unstuck: The First Steps 39
Part V:	Tools, Tips and Techniques for Prying Yourself Loose . . . 51

There are no classes in life for beginners:
Right away you are always asked to
deal with what is most difficult.

– Rainer Maria Rilke

Introduction

I always knew I had a book in me. I'd thought about writing about so many different subjects, but a book never came to fruition.

However, this book came to me one day when I was sitting around the dining room table with some friends, men and women in their 50s and 60s. A discussion started about what our plans were for the next phase of our lives. The children were grown and out of the house, several of us were going through divorces or career stagnation, some had health challenges, others faced financial problems, and several had various combinations of them all.

We talked about how we got to where we are, and we identified one thing we all had in common: None of us were doing what we had gone to college for. Most had gotten on their career path by happenstance rather than by plan. For some of us, our careers were disappearing due to new technologies; for others, it was due to the change in the economy.

For the majority of us, retirement was no longer a viable option. In fact, one of my friends said sarcastically that he would probably end up spending more time in his next career or job than he had between college and now. We agreed that a Wal-Mart-type job wasn't going to be an option. Even my friends who could retire comfortably were facing an uncertain future. For all of us, the idea of leading a life of significance and leaving a lasting legacy was a very important priority.

The one thing we all agreed on was that for the most part, we were stuck, and there wasn't a manual, instruction book, or how-to guide written specifically for us in the Baby Boomer generation for getting unstuck.

They turned to me, knowing that I am now a very successful coach, and asked how I was able to find my purpose, find a new career, be independent, and live a life of significance. It was at this moment that it all came together and I realized this was the book I was destined to write. This book will explain how you too can get unstuck, achieve what you want, and create a life that's rich and rewarding.

Based on my own journey to get unstuck, I'll explain how I changed the way I think and feel about the world, how I eliminated self-limiting doubts, discovered my true purpose, and found love in a rewarding, enriching relationship.

As some of you will no doubt recognize, many of the techniques I describe here are based on NLP (neuro-lingusitic programming). I'll teach you how to use them and apply them as needed. I know these techniques work because I've gone through the process myself and have used these techniques on my clients in my coaching practice with similar incredible results.

My mission is to transform the way you view the world, change your way of thinking, help you develop a new mindset, and guide you in getting yourself unstuck.

Part I
My Path from Being Stuck to Getting Unstuck

> "Security is mostly superstition. It does not exist in nature....Avoiding danger is no safer in the long run than outright exposure. The fearful are caught as often as the bold."
>
> – Helen Keller

Part I
MY PATH FROM BEING
STUCK TO GETTING
UNSTUCK

I promise that this book won't be all about me. This chapter describes my path from stuck to unstuck, which I realized was important to include, because it became clear to me that I'm here because of *all* my experiences–good, bad and neutral. They all had to happen in order for me to be exactly where I now find myself. This concept applies to all of us: Our successes, failures, mistakes and life lessons are all part of our journey.

Now, this doesn't mean I believe that our fate is pre-determined. In fact, just the opposite is true. I believe we have the ability to make life and career-path decisions every day of our lives. How and why I've made the choices I've made are a product of my parents, relatives and other people who had an influence on my life, as well as everyday life experiences.

I started my journey at Royal Hospital in the Bronx, New York, in June 1952.

My parents were Jewish, middle class people. Both had experienced the Depression and World War II. My father had served in the Pacific in the Seventh Army Air Corps as an officer and bombardier. He flew more than 90 combat missions and was wounded on more than one occasion. My mother finished high school and went to work. They married in 1945 and were together until my father passed away in 1989. My father was a skilled tradesman his whole life, and my mother, a housewife. My sister is six years older than I, so I've always joked that I grew up an only child with an older sister.

We left the Bronx in 1957 for suburban life in a tract home on Long Island, New York. In 1963, my parents decided that they wanted to live in a more Jewish area so that my sister could meet a "nice Jewish boy" rather than the non-Jewish boys she had been seeing. So, they moved to Long Beach, New York, where I grew up and attended school from fifth grade to graduation, with the dream of becoming--what else?--a medical doctor.

Long Beach was an extremely affluent area. All of my friends' fathers were either professionals or business owners. Many were in the garment industry and most worked in Manhattan. For me, the son of a blue-collar worker, this wasn't an easy environment to fit into.

My father was a highly skilled and sought after craftsman, so he believed he didn't have to take any guff from anyone. But he was labeled as difficult and sometimes went for weeks without work. As you might guess, money was always in short supply.

Unfortunately, I picked up his attitude: I thought, my skills would put me above the consequences of bad behavior and arrogance. But I learned otherwise, on the first three critical steps in my journey, during junior high school. The first was in the 7th grade, when I failed math; the second was when I had to go to summer school that same year for doing poorly in my English class; and the third—and most important—was being accepted into Mr. Lovely's (the person in my dedication) public speaking class in the 8th grade.

Failing math set me on a path of loving the arts; going to summer school gave me my love of the English language, vocabulary and grammar; and Mr. Lovely taught me how to stand up in front of a large group and use my abilities and knowledge to express myself and influence others.

As expected, I went to college as a pre-med major, but I quickly found out that I wasn't equipped for all the math and chemistry and I wasn't motivated (way too much partying) to do the studying or put in the effort that was required.

After much introspection and agonizing, I decided to switch my major to Teaching, then to History. And after getting grades barely good enough to graduate, off I went into the working world. As I was ill-equipped for anything in particular, I got a job in sales.

I started off at a brokerage specializing in used metalworking machinery, A&A Machinery, in my hometown of Long Beach. Here I learned how to sell over the phone and negotiate multi-thousand-dollar deals on huge pieces of equipment both in person and over the phone. And I got my first taste of business travel.

My next major career move was to Reuben H. Donnelley, as a sales agent for the New York Telephone Company's Yellow Pages. Here I found my first real success and mentors: the late Steve Stern, and the man who would significantly influence my future with his common sense and love of life, Hank Giordano.

I was good enough to become the youngest account executive at RHD in its history. I won numerous sales awards and recognitions and I made very good money, but I was still very unhappy. And I still had the attitude I got from my Dad: I said what was on my mind without thinking or caring; I always believed that I was so good at what I did that nothing could touch me. A policeman friend of mine once told me my ego was writing checks that my abilities couldn't cover!

This attitude haunted me through several subsequent positions, including my two favorite jobs: selling print advertising in a major trade publication to the meetings, conventions and trade show industries; and as a partner in a company that marketed and educated planners of military reunions.

While working at the trade publication, I was offered the opportunity to take over the Florida and Southeast regional office. My first wife,

Gina, and I transferred to Broward County, Florida, in 1988. We bought a beautiful home in Coral Springs and decided to start a family. We found that it wasn't to be; after spending many thousands of dollars, we had to give up.

This marked the beginning of the end of our marriage. After I was fired from the trade magazine, I panicked and made a series of bad career choices, each one worse than the one before. I'm not going to bore you with the details; just suffice it to say that I don't think I was meant to work in a corporate environment.

My partner's wife at the reunion company was a horror, never appreciating the time, effort, and marketing and sales creativity I was putting in to turn a bankrupt company into a profitable one. Essentially, she made my life and that of just about everyone who worked there a nightmare.

Out of nowhere, in 1999, I saw a posting for a job with a major publishing company where one of my former bosses worked. I called him, he pulled some strings, and the next thing I knew, I was moving to California with my girlfriend, Karen, who would become my wife, and her 7-year-old daughter, Lauren.

In early 2002, the tech bubble ended and so did my job. I wanted to head back to the East Coast, but Karen wanted to stay so Lauren would have stability.

In 2008, I had a near-death experience that profoundly changed my life. I knew that the life I was living was killing me. I was exceptionally unhappy. I hated what I was doing, and my marriage was headed nowhere. I began looking for any reason to get out of my home office, so when I found a Meetup group about NLP, I attended its next meeting.

That led me to a free three-day seminar on becoming a certified hypnotherapist. Little did I realize that this was the beginning of a wonderful, incredibly fulfilling career.

Karen was not supportive of my journey, and in 2010 we separated and got divorced. But since then, I've been able to follow my passion, and you, my reader, will be the beneficiary of my journey, education and knowledge. So read on, and I'll be your guide from stuck to unstuck.

To say that this has been an easy journey would be giving you false hope about what lies ahead in your quest to get unstuck. Like all journeys into the unknown, you've got to prepare yourself for every conceivable challenge, barrier, pitfall, for those inevitable twists and turns, moments of doubt and feelings of failure.

It will probably take more time than you planned and a lot more resources than you expected. Remember, make plans and budget for the worst-case scenario. Don't discount any possible problems that in your wildest dreams might occur. Be prepared for those around you to question your motives and take every chance to disparage your dreams or urge you to give up or turn back.

This is a journey out of the known and into the unknown, a journey that right from the first step takes you out of your comfort zone—which means that every decision you make, every choice you're faced with, will probably not fit into any of your past experiences. You'll find yourself questioning your identity, your values, your beliefs, your determination. And even if you don't, others certainly will.

I'm in the position to make my own decisions and not have to answer or justify myself to others, so I chose to go it alone to "Get Unstuck" and create my new life path. All I can tell you is: BIG MISTAKE!

That's right...BIG MISTAKE! Have you ever heard of any great exploration that was done by a lone man or woman?

As I muddled along, I often found myself at crossroads where I had to make choices and decisions I had never faced before. Going it alone caused me a lot of anxiety, self-doubt, and side trips that led to dead ends, costing me both time and money.

So, I did a lot of reading about great explorers, inventors and thinkers and found that they all had the following 10 qualities and behaviors in common:

1. They had a goal in mind.
2. They got information and education that was available.
3. They had a plan.
4. They found others who could provide them with expertise that they didn't have.
5. They gathered people around them who believed in them and gave them courage to keep going even when all seemed lost.
6. They found guides who could give them advice at least part of the way.
7. They kept a detailed journal of their experiences.
8. They learned from their mistakes and changed their decision-making process accordingly.
9. They were flexible in their behaviors and learned to adapt to new situations.

10. They were grateful for their trials and tribulations for having shaped them to become a very different–and likely stronger–person than they had been when they started out.

Part II
How You Get Stuck

(It isn't always your fault.)

Except for the fear of loud noises
and the fear of heights,
you are born without limits.
You decide your limits and the
beliefs that go with them.

The best news is...
you can "undecide" decisions and
unlearn those limiting beliefs
even if you're not sure when you
decided to believe them.

How You Get Stuck

Staying In Your Comfort Zone

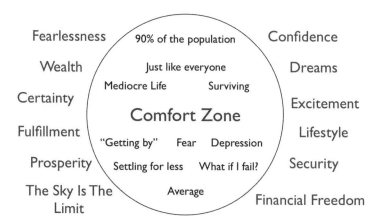

"If you accept the expectations of others, especially negative ones, then you will never change the outcome."

– Michael Jordan

Crabs in Your Bucket

When people who love you hold you back, they're called "crabs in your bucket."

Crabs in your bucket can hold you back for two reasons: their insecurity and their jealousy.

The BIG question is: How will you stand up for yourself and tell them you're worth it?

Where do our beliefs and value systems come from?

The most simple and comprehensive answer is: EVERYWHERE, EVERYTHING and EVERYONE you've ever been exposed to since birth.

Values and Beliefs

Psychologists generally agree that we acquire our values and beliefs during four key periods in our development, commonly called the imprint, modeling, socialization and adult/business-persona periods.

Imprint period, birth to 7

During this period, we are sponges absorbing everything we see, hear, feel, smell and taste, and what's critical is that all this information comes in completely unfiltered. However, it's important to note that it is also during this period that we experience our first and root encounters with the negative emotions of anger, sadness, fear, hurt and guilt. Whether we're aware of the actual causal event or moment is unimportant, because our unconscious minds record everything, store and preserve it for our entire lives.

Question to ask yourself: Who were the biggest influences in your early years? (Write the answers here)

Modeling Period, age 7-14

Around the end of age 7 and beginning of age 8 is when most children start developing the ability to think critically—that is, to make decisions about how they experience the world.

It is at this time as children that we start to look for role models, and it really doesn't matter if they come from our immediate or extended families or from outside of our direct experience. What boy growing up in America in the late 1940s through the early '60s didn't imagine being his favorite baseball player stepping up to the plate when playing with his friends? And every girl wanted to be the perfect homemaker, like Donna Reed.

I wanted to be Roy Rogers or Sky King. I dreamed of being the Rifleman, Bat Masterson, Steve Canyon or John Wayne taking on the whole Japanese Army.

I imagined myself as Wyatt Earp taking on the bad guys at the OK Corral, or Davy Crockett at the Alamo, or Sgt. Saunders (Vic Morrow in Combat) out on patrol with his squad running into a Nazi machine-gun nest.

This was when I decided, like all my friends at the time, that I was going to be a policeman, a fireman, a pilot or a doctor.

This is also the time when authority figures other than our parents began to influence our lives—primarily, our teachers.

Question to ask yourself: Who were your heroes and on whom did you model yourself? (Write the answers here)

Socialization Period, age 14-21

Those "wonderful" junior high, high school and college years, when friends and peer groups are everything you need in life.

So much of our identity and values come from the group we belong to— the "in/cool" crowd, the jocks, the nerds, the druggies, the hippies, and other groups that exist at school.

This is also where many of us first experience the differences between kids who come from families with money and kids from families with less, evidenced by clothes, cars, vacations, and which side of the tracks they lived on. These groups almost never mixed socially outside of school. And at many school functions, they were easily identifiable.

Our parents always told us not to hang out with the "bad crowd," that we would be judged by the company we kept. It wasn't until I became a parent myself that I really understood—and passed along--my parents' advice.

WHAT CROWD DID YOU HANG WITH IN...

...junior high?

_____
_____
_____
_____
_____

...high school?

_____
_____
_____
_____
_____

...college?

_____
_____
_____
_____
_____

Adult/Business-Persona Period, Age 21 and up

Here's where we learn the principles of business and mature into adults. Our identities change as we go through various transitions, becoming spouses, parents and business owners, advancing professionally, and so on.

These changes affect our values, beliefs and abilities.

Questions to ask yourself:

What changes in identity have you experienced?

_____
_____
_____
_____
_____

What new identities have you taken on?

_____
_____
_____
_____
_____

Values

1. **Values** are highly unconscious motivators that determine how we choose to spend our time.

2. **Values** affect how we feel about what we've done, so they relate to how we feel about ourselves and about others.

3. **We have different values** for the different areas of our lives.

4. **There are three types of values:**

    1. Surface: These are values that come easily to mind, but they are not always the most important.

    2. Deep: The really important values that motivate us on the most unconscious level.

    3. Threshold: These values are the ones that are deal-breakers.

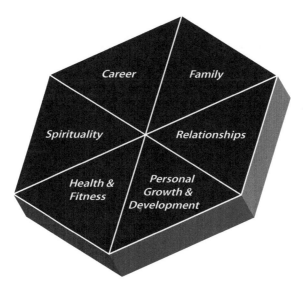

Discovering Your Values

What's important to me about the [select from above] _____ area of my life?

Order	Value

Part III
How Does the Mind-Body Connection Work?

Is it by magic? No, it's just chemistry!

Neurological Connections

There are...

$$(10^{10})^{11}$$

possible neurological connections in your body.
That's the number 10 with 10 zeros after it,
written 11 times!

100,000,000,000,000,000,000,000,000,000,000,000,000,000,000,000,000,000,000,000,000,000,000,000,000,000,000,000,000,000,000,000,000,000,000,000,000,000

The Mind–Body Connection

Physiology and Chemistry

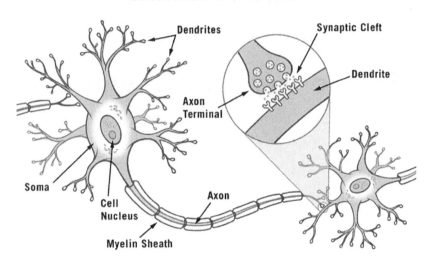

Diagram of 2 Neurons

How an impulse, thought, memory, process or reaction travels from the brain to our consciousness— or even better, how our bodies run automatically—is very complicated stuff. So rather than trying to explain it poorly, I turned to Paul D. Corona, M.D. a physician and expert specializing in this area, and his book, *Healing the Mind and Body*.

(The following is reprinted by permission of Dr. Corona. All italics are his.)

A *neuron* sends a signal through a wire-like filament called an *axon*. They *receive* messages through tiny branches (*dendrites*) that spread out in all directions. Imagine a complicated mesh of telephone lines that enable neurons to "talk to each other." A neuron sends an impulse through its axon, which is received by another neuron through one of its dendrites.

These incredibly thin wires, however, do not actually touch each other but are separated by a tiny gap known as a *synapse*. If one wire is sending information to another, something has to happen at the synapse level in order to carry that information forward. What happens is the release of a neurochemical by one wire into the gap, where it is then taken up by the other wire.

The side of the gap that *transmits (sends)* the neurochemicals is referred to as *presynaptic*. These chemicals are passed through the cell membrane by way of small holes called *receptors*. The side that *receives*, or *uptakes*, the neurochemicals on the transmitter cell is referred to as *postsynaptic*. The chemicals pass through other receptors in the cell membrane of the next neuron. Each receptor site has a specific function, and only neuro-chemicals are allowed to pass through certain receptor sites.

I'm including this next discussion so that you understand what can cause the nervous system to work improperly, from an expert medical viewpoint. I'm not qualified to offer any remedies, and I strongly recommend you seek medical attention if you're experiencing any of the conditions described here. It is my belief that in order to effect the permanent life changes you might seek, your nervous system must be balanced and healthy; otherwise, the messages and learnings you're taking in could be misinterpreted or changed. A great metaphor for this would be the game of "Telephone," where the final message, after many recitations and interpretations, turns out quite different from the original.

From Dr. Corona:

"Unfortunately, the nerve cells do not always communicate successfully across the synapse. The receptor sites the chemicals travel through should ideally transmit the chemicals in one direction—forward.

"Imbalances in the nervous system occur when the receptor sites *spring a leak,* allowing the chemicals to move in the wrong direction--backward. The neurochemicals therefore fail to pass through the nerves efficiently, causing an imbalance that affects whatever tissue is at the end of that nerve. This leakage is detrimental to the purpose and function of neurochemicals, because they are not allowed to continue the flow forward of communication from one neuron to the next."..."When many chemicals are not moving along as they should, the mental and physical breakdowns will be more numerous and more severe."

THE MIND–BODY CONNECTION

Conscious and Unconscious Minds

Why we do what we do

In psychological terms, we're really made up of two exactly balanced minds—the conscious and the unconscious—working in alignment.

Dr. Mihaly Csikszentmihalyi, Ph.D., former head of the department of psychology at the University of Chicago and now Distinguished Professor of Psychology and Management and founding co-director of the Quality of Life Research Center at Claremont Graduate University in California, wrote in his book *Flow: The Psychology of Optimal Experience* that the unconscious mind takes in 2,000,000 bits of information per second (bps) and filters them down to 126 bps of information and arranges them in groups, or chunks. Depending on the importance or complexity of the information, the unconscious may break in into 5 to 9 groupings for the conscious mind to act upon.

Do the math: The conscious mind represents .006% of mental activity, and the unconscious mind does the remaining 99.004%! This disproves the commonly held belief that the conscious mind represents 10% of your mind and the unconscious mind represents 90%.

So, you're always using 100% of your mind, but the processing is happening in a different way than you've always thought.

The Conscious Mind

> Your conscious mind is the .006% of your mind that you are aware of. It's the part of your mind that you actively "think" with.

It is aware of the environment that surrounds you; it is the part of you that is always scanning for danger. It is also aware of any bodily functions that are not functioning correctly.

It is analytical. This is where logic and rational, unemotional thought takes place.

It is critical. It decides what outside information, thoughts or ideas you will accept or reject.

It is computational. This is where all mathematics and logical processes are done.

It handles decision-making. Like a CEO, its job is to make critical strategic decisions on the 126-bps report given to it by the unconscious. It can also override the unconscious mind.

The Unconscious Mind

> Your unconscious mind contains all the thoughts and functionality of the mind that you're not aware of.

It is always active. It never sleeps. It takes in information and stimuli constantly, 24 hours a day, 7 days a week, starting prenatally in the womb and continuing until death.

It stores and organizes all your memories and learnings as a combination of pictures, sounds, feelings and internal dialogue. Also, because it stores so much information, it tends to delete, distort and generalize those memories.

It's where creativity, emotions, attitudes, beliefs, values and identity come from.

It covers up memories with unresolved negative feelings and decisions.

It sometimes brings up those memories to your conscious mind occasionally to release the negative feelings—those seemingly long-forgotten and then out-of-the-blue memories that give you an emotional twinge and then disappear.

It preserves the body. It makes sure that all bodily functions are maintained. It also directs your immune system and lets your conscious mind know when issues need to be addressed.

It enjoys serving, but it needs clear orders to follow. It wants you to succeed. It's now believed that the conscious mind sets goals and the unconscious mind achieves them.

It maintains your instincts and generates habits, better known as gut feelings and things you do automatically.

It takes everything personally. It's egocentric. So when you speak negatively about someone else, your unconscious hears it as if you are talking about yourself.

It follows the path of least effort. It wants things to be simple. It doesn't want to waste energy.

It's symbolic – it thinks in pictures, sounds and feelings.

It doesn't process negatives. For example, try not to think of a blue tree. What do you think of? A blue tree. Why? Because the unconscious mind hears "Think of a blue tree."

Now, for the purposes of getting unstuck, the most important aspects of the unconscious mind to consider are that it stores every event and memory as a combination of pictures, sounds, feelings and internal dialogue; and, because it stores so much information it tends to delete, distort and generalize those memories.

There's a saying by Dr. Milton Erickson, "the father of modern hypnotherapy," that many other well-known psychiatrists subscribe to: "If all my patient's problems are metaphors, then the cure is also a metaphor." What Dr. Erickson was saying is that the unconscious mind is really a "metaphor machine." This means that all our problems and sticking points are symbolic of what is going on in our unconscious processes.

Part IV
GETTING UNSTUCK: THE FIRST STEPS

"I work really hard at trying to see
the big picture and not getting stuck in ego.
I believe we're all put on this planet for a purpose,
and we all have a different purpose.... When you
connect with that love and that compassion,
that's when everything unfolds."

–Ellen DeGeneres

Who and What Do You Want to Be?

That's the biggest question I had to figure out. And I did, so let me give you some insight into the process I used. For some of you, it will be a quick process and the answers will come easily. For others, the road may be longer and have a few more twists and turns.

I've worked in corporate America, but I've been an entrepreneur for the majority of my career, so my basic choice was settled: Whatever I did, it would be entrepreneurial. It's important to note that many entrepreneurs just create a job for themselves, and that is perfectly alright; others build a business that generates income for them even when they're away.

I started out creating a job, and it's growing into a self-sustaining business.

Now, how to start and where to start?

I started by creating a list of everything I was interested in, no matter how far-fetched. What made this list different from my previous attempts was that I didn't just sit down one night and create it; instead, I carried a pad of Post-it notes with me and every time an idea or interest popped up, I wrote it down on a Post-it. When I got home, I'd stick the day's notes on the white board I kept in my office..

After about three months, a pattern began to emerge. I then started to arrange the notes in groups with similar themes.

Lesson #1: There is No Failure, Only Feedback.

One thing stood out: My number-one career choice was to be a coach of some sort, and considering that I'm a very good public speaker and a Distinguished Toastmaster, becoming a presentation and public speaking coach seemed a natural choice

I tried that, but after two years of time and money invested, it just didn't work out. I did learn from it, however—to be flexible and willing to make mid-course corrections.

Lesson #2: Investigate the possibilities.

There are a lot of free educational resources and opportunities available these days. Once you decide on your area of interest, search the Internet for groups related to that interest. See what education and professional certifications they offer. Listen to the members' successes and challenges. See if you can bring a new approach that's unique to you.

Lesson #3: Many success seminars are all sizzle and no steak.

At these seminars, you'll hear a lot about changing your current mindset and creating a new one. They'll teach you just enough to get you lured in to buy the 12 CD/DVD sets and workbooks and sign up for the next level at an amazing discounted package price. Usually, self-help turns into "shelf-help."

Be discriminating and don't be pressured into purchasing unless it feels right. Be patient; learn what you can, trust your instincts, and you'll know when it's the right investment for your future.

Lesson #4: Be flexible and be willing to give up the path you're taking in order to get where you need to be.

Quite often we start down a path only to get stuck at a dead end. Don't be afraid to turn off that path before you get stuck. If you do get stuck, find someone who can get you to see other alternatives and keep you going. Sometimes, you might have to backtrack, and it's comforting to know that your coach has been down a similar path before getting to his/her goal.

Lesson #5: Find a coach.

COACHING

"**Coaching,** when referring to getting coached by a professional coach, is a teaching or training process in which an individual gets support while learning to achieve a specific personal or professional result or goal...Coaching may also happen in an informal relationship between one individual who has greater experience and expertise than another and offers advice and guidance, as the other goes through a learning process." –Wikipedia

Why do you need a coach?

Ever hear the warning that becoming successful will wreck your budget and take more time than you ever imagined? This is especially true if you're trying to do everything on your own.

Where did I get this insight? I got it from every entrepreneur and successful businessperson I've ever spoken to! Each described the benefits that came from being coached: the tremendous advantage of having another point of view, being guided to solutions where none seemed to exist before, having someone to be accountable to, learning from someone who has faced similar challenges, and accessing the coach's network.

How do you choose a coach?

The best advice I've gotten is to choose your coach wisely. I advise choosing one for each area of your business or life that you want to change. That's right, as much as I tried to resist, I found that I needed different coaches for the different areas of my life and career.

The first coach I engaged was a "cheerleader," best-friend type, a shoulder to cry on, and a sounding board for my challenges and obstacles. Instead of an advisor, I got someone who really didn't move me forward. That person, though very encouraging, never challenged me to move out of my comfort zone or revise my poorly formed goals, never held me accountable for reaching my goals or called me on my excuses for not fulfilling my obligations. Simply put: That coach allowed me to remain stuck, and (at least at the time) I felt better about it!

What I finally realized is that I never really outlined in my own mind what kind of coach I needed in order to get unstuck. I had to make a commitment to myself that no matter how uncomfortable and anxiety-inducing it might be, getting unstuck would mean moving forward.

So I fired my coach and set out to find one who would push me forward, make me set realistic goals, hold me accountable, and call me on my BS when necessary. I also needed a coach who had been down the road before and could help me avoid the pitfalls and mistakes that possibly lay in front of me.

As I focused on finding such a person, I was at a three-day seminar dealing with creating public speaking seminars, and out of nowhere, my soon-to-be coach and mentor, Michael, appeared.

I knew it immediately, and my true journey to getting unstuck began.

Since then, I've taken on other coaches, each one with a different area of expertise. I now have a branding coach, a marketing coach, a book-writing coach, an accountability coach, a social media coach, and a coach to help me with my practice and my more challenging clients.

You might think this is overkill, and in the past I would have agreed with you. But I've found that having coaches who fulfill my requirements, fit my personality, and deliver what they promise has propelled me forward at warp speed, saving me a lot of time and a huge amount of money.

"With the right kind of coaching and determination, you can accomplish anything, and the biggest accomplishment that I feel I got from the film was overcoming that fear."

— **Reese Witherspoon,** on getting coaching to prepare for her role as singer June Carter in the film *Walk the Line*

Coach-Selection Worksheet:

List Your Requirements

Know Your Outcome

Decide What Type of Coach You Need:
- Success
- Accountability
- Career
- Relationships

Do your research online and in person:
- Make sure they will challenge you
- Make sure you're in sync with each other
- Go to seminars to find out what is being offered and by whom
- Be skeptical, trust your instincts, ask questions of others in the audience
- Be ready to upgrade and change coaches if you're not getting the results you desire

Group Coaching & Master-Mind Groups

Coaching can take other forms besides the one-on-one format.

As I got further along in my search for coaching, I started to realize that there were others out in the world who were just as stuck as I was and were looking for answers from others. In fact, there are whole communities looking to support and/or to be supported.

The first place to look for like–minded people is on the Internet. With a quick Google search, I found lots of groups online as well as in-person communities. of people who had the same interests and challenges.

I also checked LinkedIn, Facebook, Twitter and YouTube and found even more.

I looked for local Meetup groups and checked to see if there were any free multi-day seminars being held within driving distance. I was absolutely overwhelmed at the number of groups available to help me get on my way.

It's important to keep an open mind and explore different groups to see if they fit your needs. You may find other like-minded individuals who are looking for similar answers about how to get unstuck.

My next-level step was finding and joining a "Master-Mind" group. This can be anywhere from 2 to 8 or more people, usually business-people of different backgrounds, areas of expertise and pursuits, for one common purpose. They all work in harmony to give support to each other through ideas, encouragement, insights and resources in a noncompetitive environment.

Why did I need a Master-Mind group?

There are many reasons:

    They have been down the same or similar path before

    They have expertise in areas that I lacked

    They have networks that they are willing to share

In a Master-Mind group, there is diversity of experience

There is a high level of commitment to each member's success

It's important to note that your Master-Mind group doesn't have to be local. Many such groups hold weekly or monthly conference calls, present webinars and host LinkedIn discussion groups or private members-only Facebook pages.

Lesson #6: Keep a journal.

All great explorers, inventors, statesmen and business leaders keep one. It will keep you on track and give you a record of your decisions and the reasons you made them. It'll be a record of your daily accomplishments, even if you think you haven't had any some days. Most importantly, it will keep you from going over the same ground more than once—you may come to a fork or crossroads reminiscent of one you approached in the past, and being able to refer back to what you did before can be of tremendous help.

I also strongly recommend that you keep a separate "Gratitude Journal" and write in it every night before you go to bed at least three things that happened that day that you're grateful for. You'll find that you'll sleep better, with less worry, and wake up in a positive mood, ready to take on the day.

Lesson #7: Take action!!!

The universe rewards action. Sitting on your butt and waiting for things to come to you won't make things happen. Need I say this again...?

Take immediate and committed action!

Part V
How Does the Mind-Body Connection Work?

Is it by magic? No, it's just chemistry!

Tools, Tips and Techniques For Prying Yourself Loose

So far I've discussed how we get stuck and covered the first steps for getting unstuck.

In this section, I'll show you how to:

- Integrate the "Empowerment Equation" into your everyday life.

- Set healthy boundaries

- Release the 5 core negative emotions:

    Anger

    Sadness

    Fear

    Hurt

    Guilt

- Identify and release self-limiting decisions and beliefs

- Create the outcomes you desire

- Be able to get yourself unstuck when you become stuck

The Empowerment Equation

$$C > E$$

Being "at **C**ause" is greater than
living "in **E**ffect"

Empowerment is moving from effect to cause and operating from a psychology of excellence.

Which side of the equation are you on?

If there's an area of life that isn't working for you, it's likely that you're living "in effect" of something—the economic environment, your career, where you live—or someone—your partner, spouse, friends or boss—outside yourself, i.e., "crabs in your bucket" directing your thoughts, emotions and decisions

What does this mean to you and how do you apply it in your life?

Before I explain, I want to tell you that this is the single most important and powerful concept I learned along my path to getting unstuck. At first, it might seem a little daunting, but I promise you it's easy to understand and even easier to use.

The concept of cause is not about how you are to blame in a given situation or how you reacted. Cause means that you are the only one responsible for your feelings and reactions. It also refers to the part you played in a given exchange and, most importantly, what can you learn or did learn from it about yourself so that you can grow as a person.

One of my instructors posed it this way: Have you noticed that the same negative situations and unpleasant people keep showing up in your life over and over again? Well, that's the universe's way of giving you the same problem repeatedly until you learn to deal with it in a positive, appropriate way.

I like to call it the "Groundhog Day" effect, named after the movie of the same name. Bill Murray's cynical and nasty character experiences the same day over and over until he becomes the best person he can be.

"Effect" is not your effect on others, but rather the effect they are having on you.

Remember the "crabs in your bucket" concept we discussed in Part II? Are you living your life based on others' opinions, are or others projecting their negative feelings and self-limiting beliefs onto you?

If you hear yourself saying or thinking that it's the other person's fault, not yours, then you are engaged in being "in effect." In my coaching practice, when I'm approached by a spouse or partner who tells me that their problems in their relationships would be better if I could change the other person, I immediately know that the person making the request is not living at cause.

So, I challenge you to ask yourself, after every negative situation or person you deal with:

Am I at cause or in effect?

If you decide that you are in effect, then ask yourself, How can I be at cause?

C > E Worksheet

Situation	Cause	Effect	Be at Cause

Healthy Relationships Require Healthy Boundaries and are necessary to be at cause

All relationships require boundaries. Having solid, fair, healthy boundaries will help you have solid, healthy, fulfilled relationships.

When you give up your boundaries, you...	When your boundaries are intact, you...
Are unclear about your preferences.	Have clear preferences and act on them.
Do not notice unhappiness, since enduring is your concern.	Recognize when you are happy/unhappy.
Alter your behavior, plans or opinions to fit the current moods or circumstances of another (living reactively).	Acknowledge moods and circumstances of others around you while remaining centered (living actively).
Do more and more for less and less.	Do more <u>when</u> that gets results.
Take the truth as the most recent opinion you have heard.	Trust your own intuition while being open to others' opinions.
Live hopefully while wishing and waiting.	Live optimistically while co-working on change.
Are satisfied if you are coping and surviving.	Are only satisfied if you are thriving.
Let others' minimal improvements maintain your stalemate.	Are encouraged by sincere, ongoing change for the better.
Have few hobbies because you have no attention span for self-directed activity.	Have excited interest in self-enhancing hobbies and projects.
Make exceptions for a person for things you would not tolerate in anyone else. Accept alibis.	Have a personal standard, albeit flexible, that applies to everyone and asks for accountability.
Are manipulated by flattery so that you lose objectivity.	Appreciate feedback and can distinguish it from attempts at manipulation.

Try to create intimacy with a narcissist.	Relate only to partners with whom love is possible.
Are so strongly affected by another that obsession results.	Are strongly affected by your partner's behavior and take it as information.
Will forsake every personal limit to get what you want or the promise of it.	Integrate the things you want so you can enjoy them, but never at the cost of your integrity.
See your partner as causing your excitement/happiness.	See your partner as stimulating your excitement/happiness.
Feel hurt and victimized but not angry.	Let yourself feel anger, say "ouch" and embark on a program of change.
Act out of compliance and compromise.	Act out of agreement and negotiation.
Do favors that you inwardly resist (can't say no).	Only do favors you choose to (can say no).
Disregard intuition in favor of hunches.	Honor intuitions and distinguish them from wishes.
Allow your partner to abuse your children or friends.	Insist others' boundaries be as safe as your own.
Mostly feel afraid and confused.	Mostly feel secure and clear.
Are enmeshed in a drama that is beyond your control.	Are always aware of choices.
Are living a life that is not yours, and that seems unalterable.	Are living a life that mostly approximates what you always wanted for yourself.
Commit yourself for as long as the other needs you to be committed (no bottom line).	Decide how, to what extent, and how long you will be committed.
Believe you have no right to secrets.	Protect your private matters without having to lie or be surreptitious.

All learning, behavior and change is ***unconscious***

Understanding Your Timeline

It's been determined that your unconscious stores all memories, emotions, values, beliefs and decisions, whether you're aware of them or not, in a linear progression. Your "timeline" is an imaginary linear representation of every memory and event from the past to the present and into the future, recorded in the unconscious mind. It records events that you might not even been aware of, yet they do exist, and the unconscious mind can indicate they happened in your past.

The unconscious does not separate past, present and future. It doesn't measure time as a conscious, precise process; rather, it likes to move quickly and efficiently. What this means is that you can create <u>future memories.</u> That's right: future memories, such as events and goals. For example, if you project the successful completion of a specific goal into your future timeline, the unconscious will have accepted that completion and will do everything it needs to do for you to attain that successful completion.

Knowing this, you can eliminate any anxiety you may be feeling or anticipating about an upcoming event.

Where Is Your Timeline?

I bet if I were to ask you to ask your unconscious mind, "Where is your future and where is your past?" you'd point in a certain direction, such as front to back, side to side, up and down, or in some direction in relation to your body.

It's not your conscious, logical, thought-out answer that you want; it's your first impulse, the answer from your unconscious.

Understanding that, think of something that happened in your past and point in that direction. Good!

Now think of something that's going to happen in the future and point toward that direction.

You'll notice that your time from past to future is in a straight line (but there are always exceptions, so don't worry if yours isn't)

Experiencing Your Timeline

Timelines and Time Techniques,™ which you'll read about later in this section, rely on the process of ACTIVE IMAGINATION, meaning you actively use your imagination as you go through the exercise.

Please read the entire section before attempting this exercise, or have someone lead you through it. With a little practice, you'll find that traveling on your timeline will come easily and effortlessly.

> Go ahead and close your eyes and think of your timeline. Now, when I say timeline, imagine what it might be. Some will see a definite line; some will see points of light, others, sound or film frames. However you see it is perfect, because it's yours. Don't worry if you don't see any details; your unconscious knows they're there.
>
> Go ahead now and just float above your timeline, making sure to look through your own eyes, instead of seeing yourself floating.
>
> Staying above your timeline, turn so that you're facing the past, and just float back into the past. At the unconscious level, there is no concept of time, so your unconscious can take you there as quickly or slowly as you'd like.
>
> After floating back into the past as far as you want, turn around now and face toward the future. Go as far as you'd like.
>
> That's great! Turn around and face in the direction of your past, as you imagine it. Now, float way up into the air above your timeline. Float high enough

that when you look down at your timeline, it seems to be only an inch long. When you reach that point, just float all the way back down to now. When you're back into now, you can open your eyes

Negative Root Causes

We all have five root causes of negative emotions–that is, the first time we ever experienced these emotions–that create filters dictating how we experience and react to the world around us. These emotions are listed in order of strength and importance:

1. Anger
2. Sadness
3. Fear
4. Hurt
5. Guilt

They are like layers of an onion, each layer needing to be peeled back, starting with anger. It's the strongest of all our emotions because we use it to stuff down any unwanted feelings or experiences.

The root emotions are usually first experienced during the period from conception (neurochemicals from your mother's blood supply) through age 2. The majority of first experiences happen in the period from conception through the first year of life.

As we experience these emotions again and again, they become cumulative until the first Significant Emotional Event (SEE) becomes a part of our awareness. But the SEE isn't the root cause; it's part of a string of pearls that continues to grow unless the original knot is untied, which can be done by using the process covered in the next couple of pages.

What's incredible is that once the root cause is removed, the unconscious removes all the negative meaning attached to the events on the string. You won't forget the events; they'll just have a different--usually neutral– emotional meaning.

Discovering the Root Cause

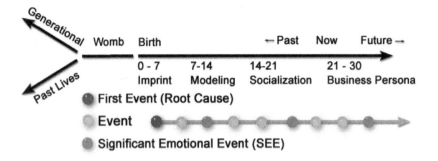

Finding the First Event

If you're stuck because of some emotion, decision or problem, it's critical to find out the root cause of it—the first event which, when disconnected, will cause the emotion/decision/problem to totally disappear.

If you already know, when was it—before, during or after your birth?

Use the following worksheets to identify possible root-cause events that may be important for your timeline. Then find the first incident of that core negative emotion so that you can release it (I explain how on page 91). After releasing the appropriate emotion, you'll see if you have the same feelings about the items on your list. They should be gone or neutral in emotional charge.

I'm Angry About...

Event	Date/Age

Finding the First Event:

- After birth: What age? _____

- In the womb? What month? _____

- During birth

- Before birth: Past life or Generational, i.e., parents, grandparents? How far back?

I'm Sad About...

Event	Date/Age

Finding the First Event:

- After birth: What age? _____
- In the womb? What month? _____
- During birth
- Before birth: Past life or Generational? How far back? _____

I'm Afraid Of...

Event	Date/Age

Finding the First Event:

- After birth: What age? _____
- In the womb? What month? _____
- During birth
- Before birth: Past life or Generational? How far back? _____

I'm Hurt About...

Event	Date/Age

Finding the First Event:

- After birth: What age? _____

- In the womb? What month? _____

- During birth

- Before birth: Past life or Generational? How far back? _____

I'm Guilty About...

Event	Date/Age

Finding the First Event:

- After birth: What age? _____

- In the womb? What month? _____

- During birth

- Before birth: Past life or Generational? How far back? _____

Releasing Negative Emotions from the Past

Understanding and imagining your timeline is essential in releasing core negative emotions and eliminating self-limiting decisions and beliefs. For this process, imagine looking down on your timeline at a key event, like this:

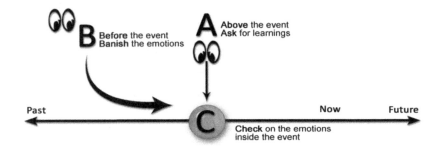

The Positions

Above the event: Above your timeline and over the past to Position A, directly above the event so you are looking down on the event. Your unconscious mind can preserve the learnings so that in the future, if you need them, they'll be there.

Before the event: Above the event and at least 15 minutes before the event, so you are looking toward now. Make sure you are well before the chain of events that led to that event. With the help of the learnings, you'll banish the emotion here.

Check in the event: To test, go down inside the event, looking through your own eyes, and check on the emotions. Are they there, or have they disappeared?!

3 Things to Check in Position B

Be sure you're doing these things in Position B when releasing negative emotions or limiting decisions:

1. Make sure you're actually in position B. Ask yourself, "Am I far enough back? Is the event below me and in front of me?"

2. Make sure you are before the first event. Ask yourself, "Am I before the first event?"

3. Make sure it is totally OK to let go of the emotion. Ask yourself, "What is there to learn from this event? If I learn this, won't it be better than having the old emotions? How can I get the same benefit that the old emotions provided when I let them go?"

What Is a "Limiting Decision"?

In general, anything that is not a negative emotion is likely a limiting decision. Here are some criteria to help you understand when a problem is the result of a limiting decision.

All Negative Beliefs: Any time a person has a negative belief about him or herself, that belief was preceded by a limiting decision that led them to that belief. If you think, "I don't deserve that" or "I don't believe I can do that" or any other limiting belief, you should ask yourself, "When did I decide that?"

All Doubts:.Similar to negative beliefs, doubts are created by some previous limiting decision. Again, if you have a persistent doubt, ask yourself, "When did I decide that?"

Comparisons: When you make comparisons such as "I wish I could make <u>more</u> money," or "All I really want is a <u>better</u> life," or "I'm not good <u>enough</u>," this should be treated as a limiting decision. When you hear yourself making comparisons, ask, "When did I decide that?"

Anything You Can't Directly Feel: When you experience and express the *negative* of an emotion–for instance, "I'm not happy," or "I just don't feel loved." When this happens, ask yourself, "When did I decide that?"

Negations: When you think in negations, such as "I <u>don't</u> make the kind of money I'd like to," or "I'm <u>not</u> lovable," or "I <u>won't</u> ever be a success," the root of it is a limiting decision. Ask, "When did I decide that?"

Any Negative Emotion Where You Find Yourself Living in Effect: If you have negative emotions for which you are in effect of something or someone else, you may have to dig for the limiting decision that created the negative emotion. Ask yourself, "When did I decide that?"

"Don't believe what your eyes are telling you. All they show is limitation. Look with your understanding, find out what you already know, and you'll see the way to fly."

– Richard Bach

Use the following worksheets to identify key events that may be important for your timeline to identify the event, whether in or out of awareness. After eliminating that belief, check your worksheet to see if the belief still exists or if there is any emotional charge attached to it.

LIMITING DECISIONS WORKSHEET

Date	Decision	

Releasing Limiting Decisions

For this process, imagine yourself looking down on your timeline, like this:

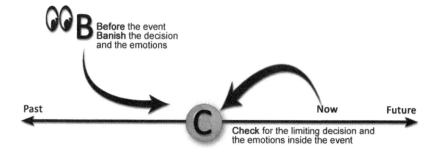

The Positions:

Before the event. Above the event and at least 15 minutes before the event, so you are looking toward now. (Make sure you are well before the chain of events that led to that event.) Your Unconscious Mind can preserve the learnings so that in the future, if you need them, they'll be there. With the help of the learnings, you'll banish the decision here.

Check in the Event. To test, go down inside the event, looking through your own eyes, and check on the decision. Is it there? Or has it just disappeared?!

Six Principles for Success

1. **Always Know Your <u>Outcome.</u>**

   - Have an idea of where you want to be and form a plan.

2. **Take Real <u>Action</u>.**

   - Don't just sit around waiting for things to happen. Make them happen. The Universe rewards action.

3. **Pay Attention to Your Results.**

   - There is no failure, only feedback. Learn from your mistakes and take corrective actions.

4. **Be Willing to Change Your Behavior.**

   - Flexibility always wins. Be willing to change your views and actions to get to your desired outcome.

5. **Always Focus on <u>Excellence</u>.**

   - Always do the best you can do. Don't focus on perfection, but rather on growing and learning. Keep in mind the adage "Your first is ALWAYS your worst!" and keep working toward excellence.

6. **Live a Life Filled with Gratitude.**

   - Make a habit of expressing thanks for what you are and what you have.

Remember...

You Get What You Focus On!

So Focus On What You Want

CPSIA information can be obtained at www.ICGtesting.com
Printed in the USA
LVOW01s1532140713

342803LV00001B/144/P